MICHAEL GALLACHER

A *carousel*
FOR MISSOULA

SHERRY DEVLIN • THOMAS BAUER • JOHN ENGEN

THE MISSOULIAN • MISSOULA • MONTANA

1

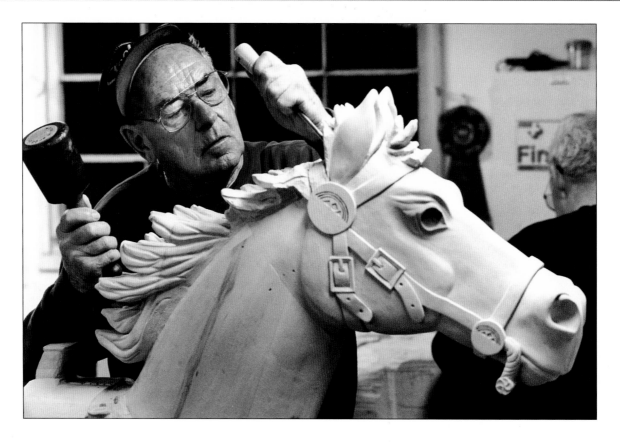

Copyright 1995, The Missoulian

Text by Sherry Devlin, except for profile of John Thompson, by Mea Andrews.
All photos by Thomas Bauer, unless otherwise indicated, except for Pony Portraits, by Ken James. Design and layout by John Engen.
ISBN 0-9634679-7-2

Thanks to our families, our colleagues, our friends and the good-hearted folks at the carousel. We're not naming names, but you know who you are.

CONTENTS

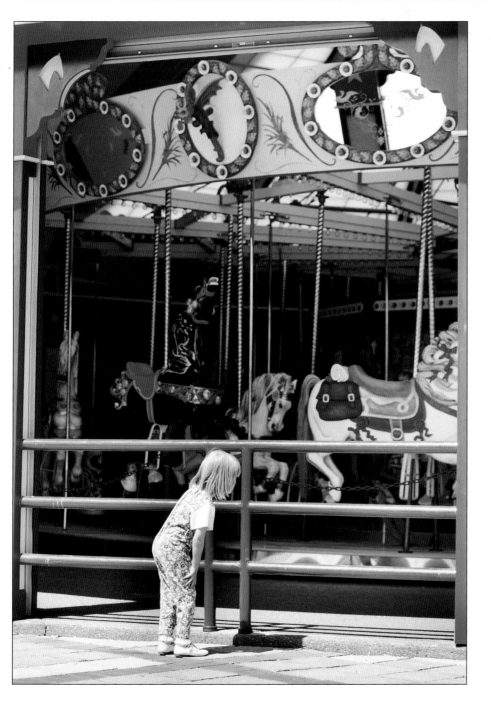

CHUCK KAPARICH'S

round trip

*t*he story of Missoula's carousel is, at the start, the story of a 19-year-old Croatian farm boy who booked passage on a steamer to America in the early 1900s, leaving behind – because there was no money – his new wife.

He made his way overland to Butte, Montana, lured by the promise of jobs in the copper mines and smelters. He found work as a smelterman in Anaconda, and – for the next seven years – saved for his young wife's passage to America.

One afternoon, many years later, John Kaparich had a portrait taken of his family. Husband, wife and seven children, the boys wearing borrowed jackets, the little girl in her best dress.

One of the photographs, he sent back home to Croatia, proof of his success and survival in America. Another was passed down, father to son to grandson.

And another afternoon, many more years later, the grandson came across the photograph and cried, realizing that his grandfather, the gruff old man who spoke broken English, had worked all his life to earn the right to call himself an American.

And Chuck Kaparich, the grandson, realized that he had never thanked his grandfather or earned for himself the right to be an American.

"My grandfather worked at the smelter every day, and grandma – when all the kids got up in the morning and went to work – would bring in a second shift of people to sleep in the beds, when they got off the shift at the mine. She ran her home like a rooming house to earn a little money," Kaparich said.

"They made wine in the basement and sauerkraut, and they would put the booze in the wagon and put a blanket on top of it and my Aunt Rose would ride on it. And the kids would deliver the booze around the neighborhood under the pretense of towing Rosie around in the wagon.

"My grandfather did anything he could to raise his family in America. And he was successful. He took that picture of those kids standing there in those suits and they didn't have two dimes to rub together. And he sent that picture home to all his relatives and he was proud."

The photograph was still in Kaparich's thoughts when he and wife Beth went to Spokane for dinner one evening in the fall of 1989. While waiting for their reservation, they walked into the Spokane carousel.

"And I just started to cry. For some people, it might be walking into a cathedral, you just get that sense of awe. But for me, it was walking in and seeing the kids spinning around on those horses," Kaparich said.

Not until he read the history of the carousel, tacked on the wall, did Kaparich realize that the horses were made of wood. "Being a woodworker all my life, I thought, 'What a piece of work.' That just blew me away," he remembered. "I went up to the horses and I touched them and felt them and I thought, 'Who would do this?' "

Then he read the wallboard telling the story of Charles I.D. Looff, the Danish immigrant who created Spokane's now-antique carousel as a wedding present for his daughter Emma.

"He was no different than my grandfather," Kaparich said. "All these people came to America. All these people like my grandfather and Charles Looff came here to be Americans. They were here to make this country something. It meant something to be an American."

Not really knowing why or where it would lead, Kaparich started studying carousels. "I just got swept away with it," he said.

He remembered his own childhood in Butte, escaping up the hill to the carousel at Columbia Gardens. Bus rides to the gardens were free on Thursdays. Bus rides to an oasis: flowers and greenery and white-sided pavilions out of sight of the dirty little mining town.

Eventually, after reading every book in the library and making at least $500 in long-distance calls to carousel historians, Kaparich called Fred Fried, an archivist and author of "A Pictorial History of Carousels."

"I thought I wanted an antique carousel horse for my front room," Kaparich said. Fried might know where best to find one.

Or might not.

Came the response from the other end of the telephone line: "You're just like the rest of those carousel vultures. You'll destroy a priceless piece of American culture just to have a horse in your front room."

"I was so fortunate I phoned a preservationist instead of a collec-tor," Kaparich said. "I went to bed that night and all this stuff kept rolling over in my head about Columbia Gardens and Spokane's carousel and all these immigrants I had read about and my grandfather. And I thought, 'You know, if they could do this 100 years ago, why couldn't someone do it today?'

"And that was when I made up my mind, lying there in bed, looking up at the ceiling, that by God I was going to build a carousel if it took me the rest of my life."

Kaparich had never even carved before. But he decided that he had read enough books and researched enough and gone to the library enough to know how wooden horses – and the carousels they rode – were built.

So he decided to build a carousel for Missoula. For his grandfather.

At noon, on Saturday, May 27, 1995, Chuck Kaparich's dream became reality. It took five years, not a lifetime, to come true.

*f*or his birthday in 1990, Chuck Kaparich got a set of wood-carving tools from his wife.

He knew so little of the craft that he didn't know to sharpen the chisels.

"Honest to God, I just bludgeoned my first horse out of wood. I think it was more determination than anything else. But I did an OK horse," Kaparich said.

It was a traditional, long-gaited carousel pony, much like an original Parker horse from 1917. Kaparich put an ear of corn behind the saddle and a sunflower on the saddle blanket, tributes to his wife's Kansas upbringing.

"And I thought, I'm going to do this. So every morning, I'd get up and carve for an hour before I went to work and come home and have dinner and then I'd work until 10 every night, making horses. It was wonderful," Kaparich said.

He carved a second pony, then another and another. A bucking pinto with a peek-a-boo mane. A graceful, armored charger. And a prancing Indian pony.

The more he carved, the more he could see his carousel sitting on Missoula's riverfront in Caras Park. In a brick and glass building, with dozens of ponies spinning under the light of a thousand bulbs.

"This was the spot where I wanted the carousel," Kaparich said. "And I thought before something else happened here, I should probably go make dibs on it."

So Kaparich loaded one of his wooden ponies into the back of his truck and went to see the mayor. "This is how naive I was. I drug this horse in the mayor's office and said I want to build a carousel for Missoula. I don't want to get paid for it or anything, but I want to make sure that it's preserved into the future and I want this little spot on the riverfront."

Mayor Dan Kemmis invited Kaparich to sit down and tell his story. Which he did. Then Kemmis said he should tell it again, to Geoff Badenoch at the Missoula Redevelopment Agency.

So Kaparich took his pony to Badenoch's office. For the first 10 minutes, Badenoch's head shook side to side: No. No. No. Kaparich kept talking until Badenoch's head changed directions: Yes. Yes. Yes.

"He just made me believe," Badenoch said. "He made us all believe."

Badenoch took Kaparich, this time with four ponies in tow, to the MRA board meeting in August of 1991. By the end of the hour, the board's chairman was threatening to climb aboard one of the steeds. Word of "the carousel man" spread the next morning on the front page of the Missoulian, and Kaparich's phone started ringing.

"People started sending letters and money and cards," Kaparich said. "We were off and running, and we had the most humble beginnings in the world."

He started toting his ponies to Caras Park on Out to Lunch Wednesdays, selling buttons for $2 in hopes of raising enough money to send a newsletter to would-be supporters and volunteers. When the first newsletter was mailed, A Carousel for Missoula had $7 in the bank.

Badenoch recruited attorney Randy Cox to organize A Carousel for Missoula Foundation Inc. and a board of directors. Cox had his doubts, but kept them to himself – and in his cautiously worded legal papers.

Kaparich, too, would wake up in the middle of the night and wonder: "Who do we think we are? We can't do this. There are too many problems. How are we going to get this part done and that

MICHAEL GALLAGHER

"This was a capital 'G' good thing. I am awestruck by the innate goodness of a lot of people in this town."

– Pat Simmons, A Carousel for Missoula Foundation treasurer, the morning after the carousel auction, April 15, 1994

part done? And it just happened.

"There were a million ways for this to fail and maybe only one for it to succeed. Somehow, it just kept funneling through that one way. When you were short of something or needed something, somebody would just show up at your door one day."

"This carousel is a study in how things come together just at the right time," said Jerry Covault, one of Kaparich's volunteer carvers and a Forest Service retiree. "You want a chariot? I'll carve a chariot. You need gears? I can do gears.

"You know that something is at work."

Covault believes the carousel succeeded, in part, because money wasn't involved. "There is pride in doing something not for money. There is pride in saying, 'Nobody can pay for this.' In a time when everything is so mercenary, nobody took advantage."

"Everyone I deal with is one of the nicest people in the world," Kaparich said. "The selfish ones don't come down to the carousel."

Wood carvers were recruited through classes at the vo-tech center – and by the growing menagerie of horse's legs, necks and heads in Kaparich's garage. Mechanics would arrive unannounced at the door. So would money, often from people who passed through Missoula en route elsewhere and caught a glimpse of a finished pony.

"The horses were our best ambassadors," Kaparich said. At shopping centers, museums, downtown window fronts, doctor's offices, schools, parties, the county fair, wherever there was an audience.

The more ponies the carvers produced, the more they all believed – and the community around them believed – that

Kaparich's dream would come true. But never, even if it meant an extra week or month or year, did Kaparich accept anything but the best.

"We are not going to rush. Ever," he told his volunteers.

It was classic Chuck Kaparich, said his cousin, Fred Dewing. "He never did anything halfway, not even as a kid," Dewing recalled. "It didn't matter if it took him 10 minutes or 10 years, he was going to build the best go-cart or the best rocket or the best model car."

"I'd go over there and they'd be making rockets out of fireworks, then rockets out of metal tubes filled with propellants. Then I'd go over the next week and they'd be remodeling the house. Nothing was halfway."

The carousel volunteers had to reach – down deep – to meet Kaparich's expectations, said Jim Dunlap, a retired dermatologist. "The real gift of this carousel was to ourselves," he said. "Every one of us found out a whole lot about ourselves that we never knew."

And along the way, Kaparich found himself. And his father and grandfather.

At Southgate Mall, just before Christmas 1993, an old man approached Kaparich, having driven all the way from Butte to Missoula to find the carousel man. "I knew your dad Johnny," the man said.

"Well that's nice," Kaparich replied.

Then came the story the man had driven to Missoula to tell: "I had never left Montana in my life, and your dad was in dental school over at Marquette. I had to get on the train and Johnny said he'd meet me at the station. It was raining cats and dogs, *cats and dogs*, and the train got delayed. The train went off the track. We got it back on the track. Finally, I pulled into the station. It was the middle of the night, it was pouring rain, the station was closed and your dad was standing out on the platform, the rain pouring on him. He was waiting there for me because he said he would."

Kaparich cried. And cries every time he retells the story. "That was my dad," he said. "Through all of this, I discover my dad. What a journey."

Kaparich's father, a dentist, died when his son was 11. "Everyone I meet says, 'You are Johnny's boy. He was a helluva guy.' "

Before he built the carousel, Kaparich had maybe three memories of his dad – the most vivid of breakfast, when mother slept late some days.

Father and son would take soda crackers and crumble them in a bowl, put sugar on top and pour coffee on top of that. "I'd eat them like cereal. Just me and my dad would sit there having breakfast together. Then he'd go to work and I'd go to school."

Had there been no carousel, Kaparich would only have had his three memories. Now he has that picture of his dad, standing in the faraway train station waiting, because he said he would, in the middle of the night. In the rain.

And he has, after all these years, after working as a cabinetmaker and before that as a gravedigger, a school teacher and a landscaper, earned the right to call himself an American.

"This really is America. This really is the greatest land in the world, when all these people can come over to Chuck's garage and build this beautiful carousel.

"I built this carousel and along the way, I kind of figured out who I was and what it meant to be an American. And I am so proud of that. I have earned a place here now. I belong here."

With John Kaparich and his son Johnny, and now the grandson, too.

❧

a pony puzzle

there have been, in carousel-making history, three styles of ponies: Coney Island (a baroque, bejeweled style), Philadelphia (a more realistic rendition) and Country (primitive).

Then A Carousel for Missoula added its own distinctive style to the genre, said Bette Largent, who paints and restores ponies for Spokane's Looff carousel (in the Coney Island tradition) and painted the lead pony for Missoula's.

The Garden City steeds are accurate, but always with a good measure of whimsy and humor, Largent said. They are sturdy, yet remarkable in their detail. The carving techniques, revealed most clearly in the head, eyes, hooves and muscles, are like no other.

"Missoula's carvers did what all artists do," Largent said.

"They created a style of their own, not a copy of something else."

Carousel creator Chuck Kaparich believes the diversity of Missoula's horses came from the decision to adopt them out to donors, who then had rights to the design.

"We weren't carving from a pattern, so the style is absolutely diverse: some classic, some funky and a little bit catch-as-catch-can. That plays out very well. There's a lot more fun in our horses," Kaparich said.

When you look at the ponies, you're looking at Missoula: the farmer's market, the construction horses, the Norwegian fjord horses, the motion and fury and color of Larry Pirnie's horse. "It's all there," Kaparich said.

"We covered a lot of territory," Kaparich said. "There is respect for the history of carousels and for Missoula, for things new and for things old. The result, I believe, is a classic carousel in every sense of the word."

Through books, trial and error, Chuck Kaparich and his carvers stumbled upon their own style of carousel pony. All volunteers, the carvers worked four nights a week, 7 to 10 p.m., in Kaparich's garage. Each horse on the carousel was carved in seven chunks: head, neck, body and legs. On the next six pages, we follow the construction of Low Bid.

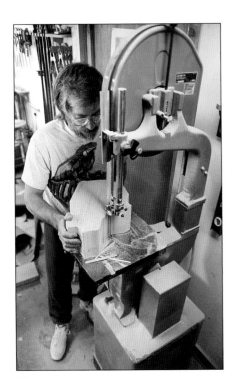

Rough cuts of ponies, whose figures were traced onto basswood from life-size drawings, were made with a band saw — the only power tool used in the creation of the carousel horses.

🐎

Built of inch-and-three-quarters-thick basswood, the ponies are the product of lots of carpenter's wood glue and a load of clamps. (A woman, walking into Kaparich's garage for the first time, once remarked: "Oh, you sell clamps for a living.") The glued pieces hardened for 24 hours before meeting the rough cut.

🐎

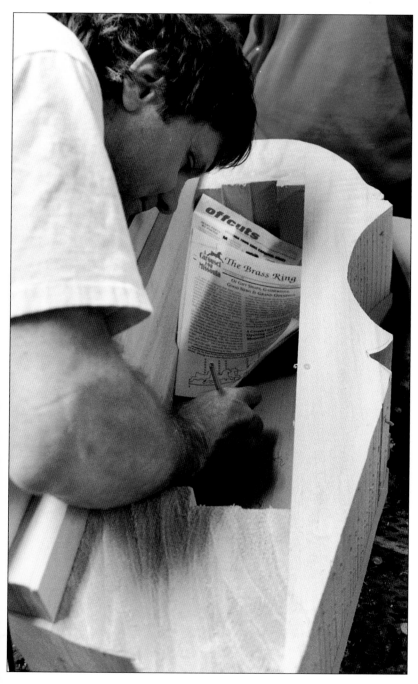

After consultation with adoptive families, a pony design was transferred from a pattern onto the basswood with a tracing wheel. Tracing-wheel lines were bolstered with permanent marker and carving began. Missoula's inside-row horses were 36 inches, rump to chest, and grew by six inches in each row.

❧

In the hollow basswood bodies of the ponies, carousel volunteers and adoptive families tucked memorabilia, including family photos, newsletters and clippings. Chuck Kaparich and his fellow carvers often signed their names inside horses.

❧

Carvers progressed like apprentices: as their skills developed, Kaparich assigned them more challenging tasks. Most moved from legs to bodies, necks and heads. "When they moved to heads, they were pretty pleased with themselves," Kaparich says. "These carvers hung in there until they got good at what they did."

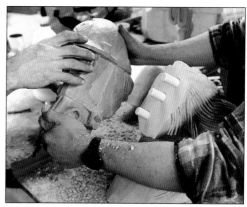

Dowels and glue went to work as pony pieces were assembled. Once the horses were whole, carvers began blending the pieces together, erasing seams by creating texture.

꙳

Before final assembly, carvers checked the fit and look of the pony pieces. Once the horse is assembled, a hole is bored for the carousel pole.

꙳

Sanders started with 80-grit paper and worked their way to 100-grit paper as they smoothed the rough edges of the carver's efforts. "The sanders should be canonized," Kaparich says, "they made us look good."

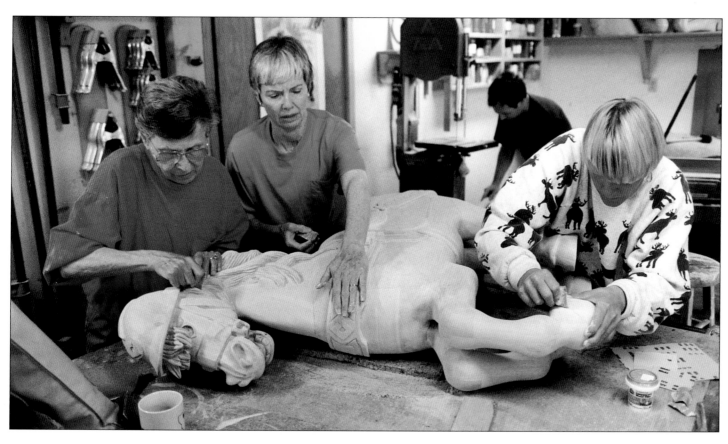

Power sanders rarely buzzed in Kaparich's garage. "The conversation would have left the room," he said. Ponies were sanded, painted with primer, sanded again, primed again and sanded a final time.

❧

Painters rarely met carvers or sanders and often worked alone. A color sketch served as a guide for their efforts. "It was a long trip from blocks of wood to the platform," Kaparich said.

❧

19

columbia belle

Columbia Belle, the lead horse on Missoula's carousel, is a tribute to the blessings bestowed upon Pat and Kitte Robins by their Irish immigrant grandparents.

"All of our opportunities for better educations, better jobs and personal freedom began with those immigrant grandparents," Kitte Robins said. Thus, the American flag tucked under Columbia Belle's cinch. And the Irish green saddle blanket and bridle bedecked in shamrocks.

As the lead horse on the carousel, Columbia Belle is the most embellished. Its halter is fitted with two 100-year-old jewels – one red, one blue – donated to A Carousel for Missoula by historian Fred Fried.

The angel behind Columbia Belle's saddle is a tribute to Mary Robins and Mary Keane, mothers of Pat and Kitte. Both women died the year the family designed their horse.

"Angels can also symbolize miracles and the spirit that makes the unbelievable believable," Kitte said. "To us, the carousel project was a miracle project."

The horse's name is a tribute to Columbia Gardens, the carousel the Robins rode as children in Butte and which burned on Pat Robins' birthday in 1973. "We consider this horse a direct descendant of the carved wooden horses at the Columbia Gardens," Kitte said.

Everyone who was ever a child in Butte experienced such sadness when Columbia Gardens burned, she said. "We didn't understand that as long as those horses were alive in Chuck Kaparich's imagination, they weren't completely destroyed."

Carver Steve Weiler was given the honor of carving the lead horse, his second pony carved entirely on his own. Bette Largent, an artist at Spokane's Looff carousel, was given the painting assignment, a thank you because she taught Missoula's carousel painters their craft.

Weiler did leave a "signature" on Columbia Belle: One of the shamrocks, he changed to a four-leaf clover. Another he used to disguise his children's initials.

ॐ

UNQUOTE

"*Chuck and Beth Kaparich are miracle people.*"

**– Kitte Robins, adoptive parent
of Columbia Belle**

21

Zonta

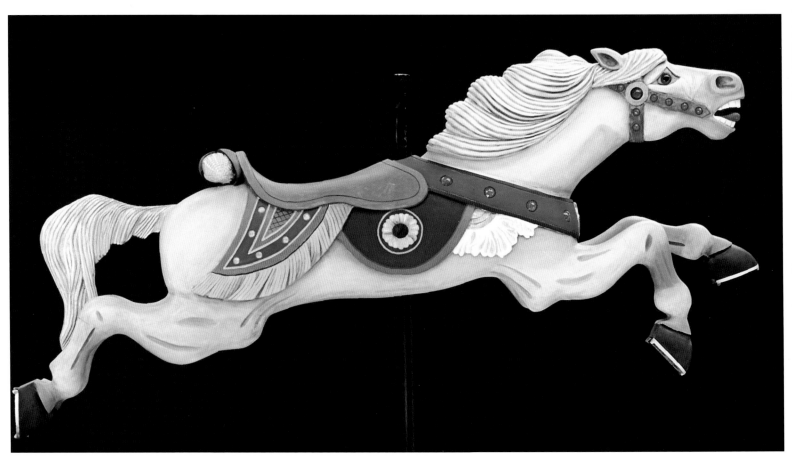

Carver Kaparich
pays tribute
to his wife
with this
traditional pony

*t*he first wooden horse carved by Chuck Kaparich, Zonta is a traditional Parker-style carousel pony that pays tribute – in its carved embellishments – to Kaparich's wife.

Beth Kaparich grew up in Kansas; thus, Zonta's sunflower-adorned saddle blanket and the corncob behind the saddle horn. Beth's son, Rob Taylor, got his art degree at the University of Kansas and painted the pony – at mom's request.

"We blackmailed him," she said.

Zonta was named and adopted, after it won the hearts of Missoula political and civic leaders, by the Zonta Club of Missoula. The club is a national organization of professional women. Its Missoula chapter was chartered in 1961.

Dwindling membership led to the group's disbanding. But members still meet informally for social, educational and professional purposes.

After carving Zonta and three more ponies, Chuck Kaparich began inviting carvers-to-be into his garage for training and then production of the remaining horses.

Beth Kaparich enjoyed the chaos. "I'm a prairie dog," she said. "I like all the people around."

❧

UNQUOTE

"*It's been exhausting, no doubt about that. But fun exhausting.*"

– Beth Kaparich, carousel volunteer and wife of carousel creator Chuck Kaparich

lil' buck

• • • • • • • • • • • • • • •

bronco's based
*on memory
of child's wild ride*

*l*il' Buck is the Montana bucking bronco carved and carried around town by Chuck Kaparich as he recruited volunteers to his cause midway through 1991.

Scott and Kim Cooney adopted Lil' Buck after it was finished, but "wouldn't have changed a thing," Kim said. "Buck is a great representative of Montana and our family."

Kim said the Cooney pony is "happy and full of spunk. He loves little kids and loves to buck. He lives to bring happiness to all. But hold on tight!"

Kaparich carved the horse, in part, in remembrance of a bucking bronco he rode as a child on the Columbia Gardens carousel in Butte. "Jet," he said, gave him a fright the first time he spun around the pole. But "cowboy's honor" kept him in the saddle.

In a poem he wrote during the Missoula carousel's carving, Kaparich remembered that first ride this way:

"I closed my eyes and screamed for help. Old Jet he seemed so wild. I held on tight through all my fright. And still my dad just smiled.

"I didn't know it at the time, but someone cast a spell. 'Cause even after 40 years, I love that carousel."

❧

avalon

pony's history
and name are
the stuff of legend

Chuck Kaparich fell in love with an armored (albeit wooden) pony one summer during a ride on the Kit Carson County Carousel, 18 miles from the Kansas border in the small town of Burlington, Colo.

The antique carousel is one of six operating in the United States in full, original paint – having been built in 1905 by the Philadelphia Toboggan Co. and originally shipped to Elitch Gardens in Denver.

When, several years later, Kaparich carved the first horses for Missoula's riverfront carousel, he modeled one after the armored charger in Kit Carson County.

Black with silver armor, Avalon was born.

As one of his first creations, Avalon accompanied Kaparich as he made his pitch to the city and its redevelopment agency in late summer 1991. Among those who heard the spiel was Pat Simmons, then director of the Missoula Downtown Association.

"I fell in love with the armored pony and told Chuck I wanted to help make his carousel dream come true," Simmons said.

When she retired in 1992, her friends adopted the pony in her name. She, in turn, gave the pony the name Avalon, not only for the mystical Arthurian isle, but for the neighborhood in Chicago where she grew up.

"This pony is dedicated to fantastical childhood adventures and dreams," Simmons said. "Fate brought this pony to me."

❧

star boy

missoula moms
team up
in a steed deed

Star Boy was one of the first four wooden horses carved by Chuck Kaparich and carried from office to office, uptown to downtown in his quest for converts.

The horse – an Indian pony replete with feathers, beads and tassels – had already been carved when four friends decided to recruit a group of working mothers to adopt a carousel horse. Their numbers quickly reached 25, with each mom donating $100 to the Adopt-A-Pony campaign.

The moms, by the way, included first-time moms, grandmothers, career moms and moms whose careers are in the home. "We never even all met each other – yet," said Ann Andre, who organized Moms for a Carousel with Missoulian co-workers Mea Andrews, Lynn Schwanke and Sharon Schroeder.

The mom "recruits" included Theresa Johnson, Sara Burlingame, Kathleen Schwanke, Virginia Braun, Diane McInally, Ann Hubber, Cindy Ondrak, Lori Nelson, Nancy Stoverud, Deb Frandsen, Anne Murphy, Lori Jacobson, Paula Lamey, Exie France, Kit Blake, Pam Volkman, Laurie Chapeski, Carla Hilleboe, Katie Apel, Ann Muncey and Felicia Saunders.

The pony's name came from "The Legend of Star Boy," a story several in the group read their children at bedtime.

Star Boy was one of four horses painted by Chuck Kaparich's stepson, Rob Taylor. "Beth and I would bribe him with tuition money for college," Kaparich said. "I ended up with four beautifully painted horses and Rob ended up with a college degree. A good trade."

❧

"*I've been a woodworker as long as I can remember, so the opportunity to create something lasting, beautiful and full of our heritage didn't have to knock twice.*"

– Chuck Kaparich, carousel carver and creator

meriwether

••••••••••••••

named for a
famed explorer,
penny pony bucks

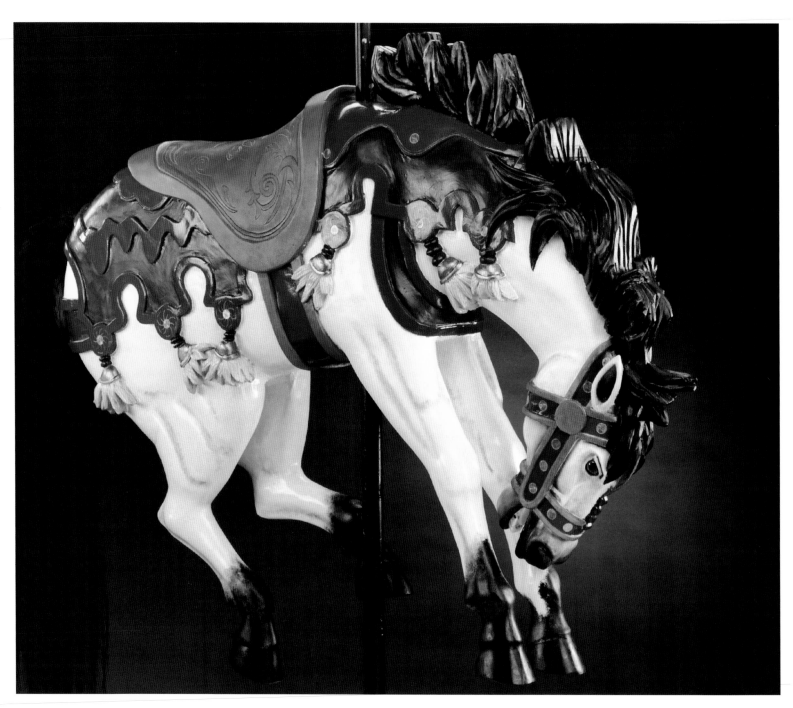

*t*hey counted. And combined. And called upon their knowledge of decimals, fractions, calculators and charts.

Then they went home and did laundry and cleaned cupboards and weeded the lawn and did more laundry to earn another handful of pennies to take to school. To count and chart.

When they were finished, Missoula school children had collected nearly one million pennies, enough to adopt four horses on A Carousel for Missoula. Each of the top-collecting classes won the right to design a horse.

The Pennies for Ponies campaign was the brainchild of Missoula teachers Jeanne Brabeck and Pat Thane, who are also wife and husband. The idea came to Brabeck as her class was studying the Bill of Rights, considering the rights and responsibilities of citizenship.

Participating teachers had their children collect pennies in gallon milk jugs. Missoula Federal Credit Union did the counting. At campaign's end, the collection weighed three tons.

Margaret Scott's 1991-92 third-grade class at Lewis and Clark School collected more pennies than any other classroom: 48,316.

Their penny pony was named Meriwether, in honor of the explorer Meriwether Lewis (one-half of the pathfinding duo for whom their school is named). Meriwether the Penny Pony is an ornately clad bucking bronco, white with a black mane.

Look closely on Meriwether and the other penny ponies and you'll find – appropriately – pennies tucked into the wood.

❧

"*I did the laundry. I cleaned the cupboard. I weeded. I did more laundry. I did more weeding. I did more laundry.*"

**– Jenna Robertson, in 1992
a Lewis and Clark School third grader
in Margaret Scott's
winning Pennies-for-Ponies class**

moonlight

penny pony
gives carousel
circus atmosphere

*h*olly Raser gave her fourth graders a gift unlike any other late in the spring of 1992: You may each, she said, select one detail to be added to a pony on Missoula's carousel.

Their collaboration was Moonlight, the carousel's circus pony. It has feathers, leg bands just above the hooves, a brilliant pink plume for a top-knot, baubles, bangles, ribbons and bows.

Raser's students at Target Range School took third place in the Pennies for Ponies campaign, collecting 34,346 pennies and rights to the design of a carousel pony. Their creation was a favorite of carvers:

Loren Stormo took three of the horse's legs on a camping trip to the Canadian Rockies during July of 1993. Campground picnic tables make excellent carving benches, he reported, although the soggy weather forced him to rig a tarpulin over his tools and basswood.

More than anything, though, Stormo found himself spreading word of A Carousel for Missoula to his campground neighbors.

For Rebecca Swindle, Moonlight was her reward for three hours every Tuesday night, after a commute from her home in Victor to the makeshift carver's workshop in Chuck Kaparich's university district garage.

The bauble holding the large feathers on Moonlight's neck carries Swindle's "signature" – the turkey track brand that her husband uses as a ranch brand.

Carver Jim Evans added his own signature to the tiny – but plentiful (74) – feathers that line Moonlight's saddle blanket. In place of two feathers, he placed fiddles, tributes to his granddaughter Candice, a state fiddle champion, and great-granddaughter Julia, a state fiddle champion-to-be.

Evans loved the whimsy of the pony. "The schoolchildren's imagination must have been at the circus the day they designed Moonlight," he said.

🐌

"I can't identify about half the pony parts I carved. When we glued all the parts together and the sanders and painters finished their work, I discovered that my contributions blended quite anonymously with everyone else's."

– Loren Stormo, carousel carver

Feathers and fiddles decorate Moonlight.

sir franklin

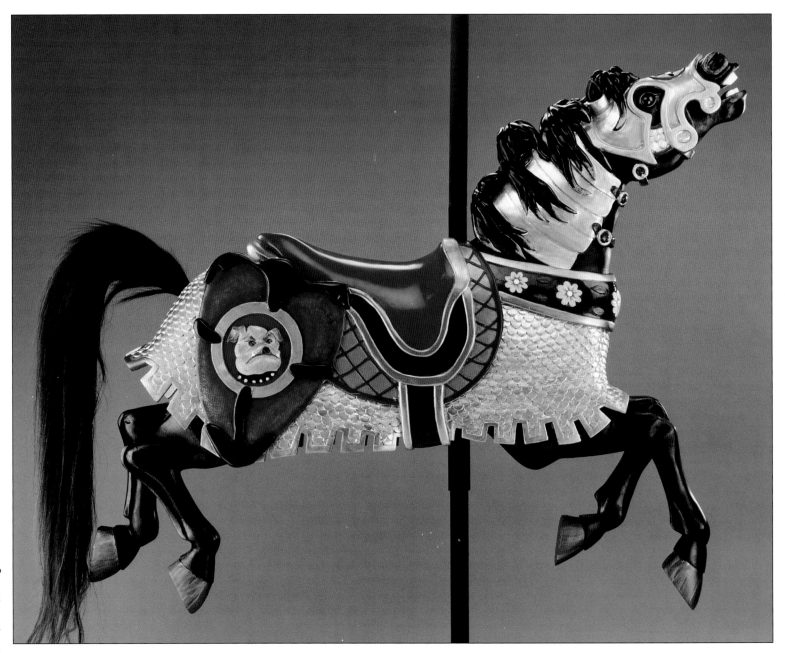

pennies brought
school mascot
to the carousel

Sir Franklin is an armored charger, a penny pony and the pride of Missoula's Franklin School.

June Brown's 1991-92 fifth-grade class at Franklin collected 43,324 pennies to win second place in the Pennies for Ponies campaign – and rights to design their own carousel horse.

Carrying young knights along the carousel's middle row, Sir Franklin displays the Franklin School mascot – a mighty bulldog – on its shield.

Look, too, for the pennies hidden in the charger's trappings.

Missoula teachers Jeanne Brabeck and Pat Thane organized the Pennies for Ponies collection, which netted $10,000 for the carousel, one penny at a time. "We just wanted to stress that kids can make a difference," Brabeck said. "And, wow, what a difference!"

The body of Sir Franklin was carved by Mike Wehmeyer. "Mike took the horse home to work on it," said carousel creator Chuck Kaparich.

"He returned it carved when we were set up in the mall during Christmas. Everyone's mouth just dropped open when we saw how beautifully the armored scales were executed. It was absolutely inspiring work."

❧

"*What really was good was our kid power.*"

– **Gabriel Nottingham,
Pennies for Ponies contributor**

35

snapples

Penny pony
has Lolo kids
at its core

S ally Nelson loves apples. And fourth graders love Sally Nelson. Little wonder, then, that the carousel pony designed in 1992 by Nelson's Lolo School fourth graders was a black-and-white pinto adorned with shiny red apples. Apples on the bridle. Apples on the back of the saddle. Some whole, some snacked on.

The students christened their creation Snapples, short for "Sally Nelson's Apples."

Nelson's class won the honor of designing a pony by collecting 19,039 pennies in the Pennies for Ponies campaign – an effort that coaxed Missoula-area school-children into contributing nearly a million pennies to A Carousel for Missoula.

Carousel creator Chuck Kaparich and artist John Thompson visited each of the four winning Pennies for Ponies classes and helped students design their horses. The only proviso: each horse had to have real pennies tucked into its trappings.

"Only schoolchildren could come up with a horse and name like Snapples," remarked volunteer Jim Evans, who carved the pony's body. "I poked along and sweated over the eagle on the front (the Lolo School mascot), but I really enjoyed doing the apples – especially the ones with parts missing."

🍎

The fruit on Snapples shows signs of snacking.

red ribbons

newspaper history
is its mane
attraction

Late in August 1870, a four-horse team left Helena pulling a wagon. The cargo: a printing press for Missoula.

Joseph and W.H. Magee, brothers, planned to start a newspaper on ground they owned in the fledgling town. But the only available press was in Helena – and the only means of transport by horse and wagon over the Continental Divide.

When, after four days, they reached Hellgate Canyon, Joe Magee pulled the horses to a stop and tied red ribbons to their ears. Missoula's first printing press, he proclaimed, would arrive in high style.

When, 120 years later, a carousel came to town, the Missoulian decided to pay tribute to Magee's press-toting horse team by adopting a wooden pony and decorating its mane with red ribbons.

The story had been preserved in John Toole's history, "Red Ribbons: A Story of Missoula and Its Newspaper." Now the carousel pony would bring the tale to life.

Red Ribbons, as the pony was named, was painted white to represent a newspaper page. Then came the silver mane and the red ribbons. A rolled – and wooden, of course – newspaper fit snug behind the saddle.

The Missoulian was one of the first businesses to adopt a horse on the carousel. Much of the carving was completed in a downtown storefront at Christmastime, making Red Ribbons one of the project's earliest and most recognizable ambassadors.

For those who collect carousel trivia, Red Ribbons is the only horse on Missoula's carousel with one ear forward and one ear back, said carver Steve Weiler.

"There has been much discussion about whether horses ever do that," he said. "But I finally found a photograph that proved it possible."

Weiler said he tried to create a "fabric flow" in the mane and ribbons. One ribbon even curves under the mane and back out again. "The curves had to be convincing," he said. "And enduring."

❧

"*Red Ribbons is a little girl's horse. My girls say it's because they like ribbons in their hair, too.*"

– Steve Weiler, carver

silver

p*ony has its roots in the Smith River and bears a carved symbol of the sea*

When, as chairman of the Carousel for Missoula Foundation, Randy Cox helped create the Adopt-A-Pony fundraising campaign, his thoughts immediately turned to a real pony – a three-quarters quarterhorse named Silver.

Silver was Cox's horse when he was growing up on a ranch near Cascade. Photographs of the "real" Silver provided the inspiration for the carousel pony Silver, adopted by the Cox family. The horses look remarkably alike.

The yellow sweet peas across the wooden pony's rump are reminders of the flowers that grow wild each spring in the Smith River and upper Missouri River country. They are also, Cox said, reminders of his courtship with wife Theresa – to whom he would deliver bouquets of sweet peas.

"Worked every time," he said.

The three J's on Silver's stirrup are in honor of the Cox children: Jason, Jessica and Jamie. The pocket on the side of the saddle matches a pocket on Randy Cox's old saddle. Its intent: to hold fencing pliers.

Look closely at the pony's trappings and you'll also find one tiny, gold-etched seashell. That is carver Chuck Kaparich's tribute to sander Ione Briedlander, who immigrated to Missoula from Florida just as the carousel campaign began and promptly donated three nights a week to the effort.

Silver was a favorite of carousel carvers, with much of the work completed at Southgate Mall over the Christmas holidays, 1993.

While carving the pony's front legs, Jim Dunlap asked Cox about the "real" Silver. "They grew up together," Dunlap remembered. "Whenever Randy described his horse, his eyes sparkled and danced, and he spoke with the same respect as one would of a good friend."

"I did my very best to place that degree of motion, strength and liveliness in Silver's posture and attitude," Dunlap said. "Randy and Silver must have been a helluva pair. I'd like to have known them back when."

&

"*Chuck Kaparich handed me Silver and told me he wanted five or six sweet peas carved across the rump. I couldn't believe what he was trusting me to do on this beautiful pony. And when I completed it, I couldn't believe what I had done.*"

– Mike Winz, carver

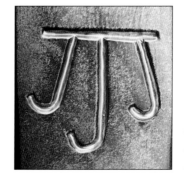

Silver's three J's honor the the three Cox children: Jason, Jessica and Jamie.

sleipnir

norsk horse
was assembled
like a fjord

Sleipnir, the adopted pony of Normanden 424, Sons of Norway, pays tribute to the Norwegians who worked in the woods and sawmills of early day Montana. And to their descendants in the industry today.

The pony is a Norwegian Fjord horse, a breed rare in Montana and distinguished by its tightly cropped mane and black stripe down the center of its back.

Most striking is Sleipnir's intricate rose-malled saddle blanket and harness, the creation of Christie Listerud, a member of the Lodge and folk artist.

Normanden 424 came to the carousel by way of Rolfe and Sharon Tandberg's visit one summer afternoon to the carousel's booth at Out to Lunch in Caras Park.

The Tandbergs were just back from a Nordic Fest and Norwegian Fjord Horse Show in Libby. The carousel's Adopt-A-Pony campaign, they realized, was a natural for their Sons of Norway lodge – which was looking for a cultural project.

"We are so proud," a lodge member later told carousel creator Chuck Kaparich.

❧

UNQUOTE

"*The first horse I rode was that big Norwegian horse – I call him 'Sven.' That horse took my eye when I saw it carved.*"

– David "Mac" MacInnes, carousel mechanic

hard hat

Carver crafts
a builder's horse
that's anything
but 'plane'

With its adoptive family in the construction business for four generations, Hard Hat the carousel pony had a history to uphold. Thus, the block plane behind its saddle, saw on its rear flank, carpenter on the front flank and brickwork on the straps.

"In the carving shop, Hard Hat was referred to as the plain (er, plane) sawhorse," said carver Steve Weiler. "But it is no plain horse."

Hard Hat, adopted by Pew Construction Co. in memory of George R. "Dick" Pew, is a tribute to the building trade.

And to Weiler's skill as a carver. In fact, the Pew family was so taken by Weiler's work that they made a donation to the carousel in his name.

Hard Hat was Weiler's first full horse to carve. "The angle of the head gives this horse such a great attitude," he said. Most difficult of the details? The face of the carpenter.

❧

UNQUOTE

"The carousel is fun at its funnest!"

**– Randy Cox, president,
A Carousel for Missoula Foundation**

A carpenter's plane rides the back of Hard Hat's saddle.

freya

norse goddess
lends her name
to this beauty

two Norwegian Fjord horses that pasture near Lolo were, by happenchance, models for the carousel pony named Freya.

The adopted pony of Hilsen 520, Sons of Norway, Freya is also a Fjord horse – a distinctive breed known for its tightly cropped mane and the black stripe down its back and through the tail.

When carver Alex McDonald was given responsibility for producing Freya, he remembered the two Fjord horses he and his wife spotted while driving near Lolo one afternoon. As he carved the carousel horse, he often drove to the Bitterroot to watch the real horses prance and play.

Freya, whose saddle blanket is a Norwegian flag, is named for the Norse goddess of love and beauty. In mythology, Freya is a beautiful blonde, blue-eyed young woman who claimed half of the heroes slain in battle and carried them to her realm in Asgard.

Friday is named for the goddess Freya.

The carousel pony Freya is also a young filly, full of energy and life. The design is that of carousel artist John Thompson, who consulted videos and photographs to put the pony on paper.

❧

"*The Fjord horse is a beautiful, beautiful breed.*"

– Alex McDonald, carousel carver

"*And the artist, carvers and painters did a beautiful job of creating our Freya.*"

– Billie Blom, Hilsen 520, Sons of Norway

dispatch

pony Express
inspires
this quick carrier
on the carousel

*d*ispatch is a Pony Express horse; its name speaks to its speed in making the appointed rounds.

Sun Mountain Sports adopted this dapple gray pony, intent on a frontier theme. To ride for the Pony Express was a dream of many on the frontier, although realized by few. The elite carried only their mail bags, bugle, Bible, Colt .45 revolver and courageous spirit.

The Express was an entrepreneur's brilliant idea – a new way of doing business. Missoula's Sun Mountain Sports seeks to be the same in the golf industry.

Carver Jim Evans fashioned the wooden pony's body (and baked cookies for his fellow carvers). "This was the last horse I worked on," he said, "and we were all looking forward to the grand opening."

"Most of the carvers on this project liked to do both sides of the horse, not just the romantic side," Evans said. "That is one of the many reasons why our carousel is and will always be one of a kind."

Carousel creator Chuck Kaparich said Evans was "like my dad. Each day when I came home, Jim would be out in my shop carving on a pony. He'd have taken all my messages, fixed the shop stools and repaired the toilet so I wouldn't have to jiggle the handle anymore."

❧

"I carved the left rear leg of Dispatch, my first carving assignment after graduating from sanding. I believe I have the dubious distinction of taking longer than any other carver to finish a single leg. I was so afraid I'd make a mistake!"

– Ginnie Morey, carousel carver

bogie

anniversary gift
is anything but
par for the course

*b*ogie was an anniversary gift from Keith to Enes (and Enes to Keith) Wright. And a gift from both to the town they love.

Keith, a golfer, chose the horse's name – for obvious reasons and because a friend's grandchild gave Keith the same nickname.

"We wanted a lively, energetic-looking horse," Enes said. "I chose Bogie's colors to match those of a horse my sister once owned."

In its trappings, Bogie carries the symbols of the Wrights' favorite activities: drama masks for theater, the treble clef for music, books in the saddlebag and an artist's pallet for reading and the visual arts, the golfer on the saddle blanket for – well, you know by now.

Bogie's tail was donated by a Stevensville woman whose favorite horse had died. "We thought it was extra special that our horse was honored with a 'local' tail," Enes said.

Bogie was carved by Bob Salo.

❧

UNQUOTE

"Where does resolution come from? Why do the right people come forward at the right time? Why now? Why do people give their time and money? Something metaphysical is at work!"

– Jerry Covault, carousel carver

toyo

• • • • • • • • • • • • •

pony pays tribute
to son, husband
and friend

*t*he "real" Toyo was a quarter horse and Tom Sherry's companion each time he ventured into the woods. Tom's mother, Minnie Weaver, and widow, Joy Sherry, wanted the carousel pony Toyo outfitted just as Tom did his bay.

Tom Sherry died in January 1991; Toyo the carousel horse is his memorial.

"I knew Tom and sometimes rode with him on horseback trips," said carver Phil Bain. "It was very special to carve the head on the wooden Toyo since I accompanied Tom when he rode the real Toyo."

Alex McDonald, who carved the horse's body, borrowed his granddaughter Alexa's western saddle to use as a model. It was, he said, made in the same style as Tom Sherry's saddle.

Tom's initials T.E.S. are carved into the horse's saddlebags.

Toyo was the first horse that volunteer carver Barry Swidler worked on. His assignment: the back right leg. "I had worked diligently on my mirror frame (a prerequisite for new carvers) expecting to slow down once I was allowed to work on a horse," Swidler said.

"I was wrong. I continued to be driven by the excitement of the project itself, as well as trying to do my small part to help it toward completion."

❧

soro

horse pays
homage to a pair
of carvers

Soro, the carousel pony adopted by Soroptimist International, is modeled after an old-fashioned Stein and Goldstein carousel horse.

With its green streamers and frilly trappings, Soro is one of the Missoula carousel's most fanciful horses. And most ornate, said Mike Winz, who carved the body.

"All of the carvers started on this horse at the same time," he remembered. "After two and a half months, the head and all four legs were done, and Chuck (Kaparich) was getting anxious to get the horse on a pole."

But Winz only had one side of the body roughed out.

"After four months, I started to get razzed pretty bad by my fellow carvers," Winz said. "Finally, after about six and a half months, Soro was ready for assembly."

Carver Barry Swidler also needed six months for his work on the neck and mane, intent as he was on staying true to the style of Stein and Goldstein – Jewish carvers known for their elaborate 1930s-era carousels.

"Being of Jewish decent myself, I felt a special connection in trying to replicate their carvings of detailed and spirited horses," Swidler said.

"*I suspect, like many other volunteers, my involvement with the carousel may be the most fulfilling project of a lifetime. I was given a chance to be part of a miracle.*"

– Barry Swidler, carousel carver

rubie

f*amily pony asks, 'tennis, anyone?'*

Rubie the carousel pony pays tribute to the Rubie family: their heritage and hobbies.

Adopted by Mike, Vickie, Ryan, Mykal and Brette Rubie, the horse is distinguished from all others on the carousel by the tennis balls on its breast collar, testimony to the family's love of the game.

Mike and the children asked that the pony "gallop" around the carousel, as Mike once enjoyed roping and riding. The horse's black shine is reminiscent of a steed Vickie rode as a child in Butte.

That horse, too, was on a carousel – at Columbia Gardens.

Look on the strap around the rear flank of Rubie and you'll find the initials of each Rubie family member. Look on the saddlebags and you'll find a fistfull of dollars – wooden ones, sadly enough. They symbolize the banking businesses Mike's father and grandfather started on the Hi-Line.

"When deals were made on a handshake," Vickie remembered.

She said all in the family wanted red rubies on the bridle – "just because."

❧

prince

neighbors pitch in
to sponsor
a royal addition

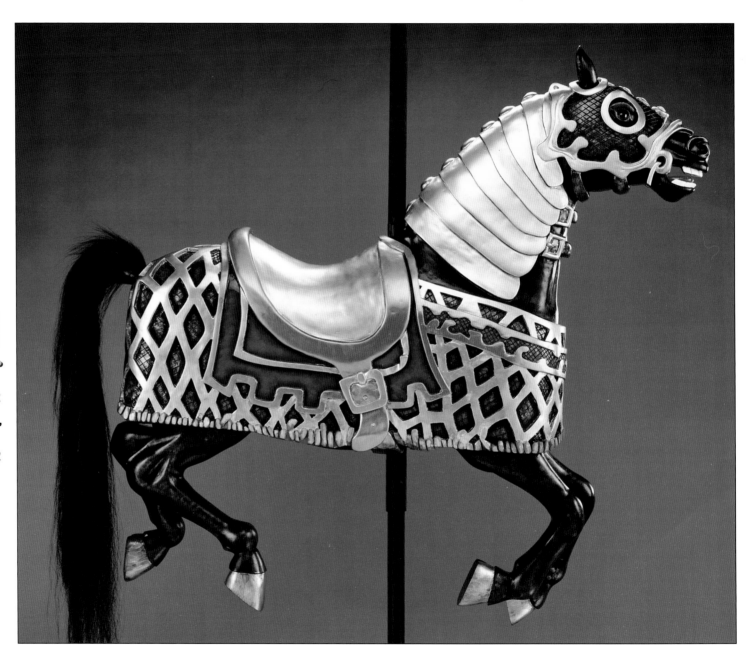

Clark Fork Riverside residents had the best seats in Missoula for marking progress on the carousel.

"We have been interested in this carousel since the first day," said 82-year-old Frances Shuey, a week before the grand opening. "We watched the roof go up. We'd see the new horses being carried inside."

Their retirement apartments only one lot down the Clark Fork River from the carousel, the Riverside residents asked early on if they could adopt a carousel pony.

A committee of tenants chose the name Prince, the armored charger design and the royal blue-and-gold color scheme.

Then they all watched as their pony took shape and then its place on the platform.

Shuey was among the Clark Fork Riverside residents who visited the carousel building a week before opening day for the hanging of the lead pony, Columbia Belle. Accompanying her was 87-year-old Teresa Hoffman.

"Excuse me," Hoffman said after Kitte Robins took a first, slow spin around the carousel on the horse she and her husband had adopted. "Is it hard to get on?" Hoffman pointed at the circle of ponies.

"No. Not at all," Robins replied.

"Because I want to ride one of those," Hoffman said.

❧

"We have admired and admired."

– Frances Shuey,
Clark Fork Riverside resident

orchard belle

Club's horse
has detail down
to the last straw

Orchard Belle may wear the only wooden straw hat in the country.

Belle is the carousel horse adopted and designed by the Orchard Homes Women's Club, Orchard Homes Country Life Club and Orchard Homes Social Circle. (The Country Life Club dates to 1911.)

Its unique look – "straw" hat, blinders, fresh vegetables behind the saddle, cut flowers on the trappings, are in honor of the truck farms that once provided a livelihood for residents in the neighborhood west of Missoula.

Carver Jim Evans lived on Short Street, in Orchard Homes, for some of his childhood and remembers the commerce well.

Orchard Belle was the first carousel horse Evans took the lead on, after having carved many, many, many pony legs and treating his fellow carvers to many, many, many dozens of homemade cookies.

"I think this is the most beautiful horse in the world – naturally," he said when Belle was completed.

While riding Orchard Belle, look for carver Evans's likeness on the painted panels that surround the carousel centerpole. (His is the face on the bag of cookies.)

UNQUOTE

"This community has done something that no other has ever done, anywhere in the world."

– Randy Cox, president,
A Carousel for Missoula Foundation,
on opening day, May 27, 1995

norm

here's a horse
with fraternal
instincts

*t*here is no other pony like Norm on Missoula's carousel. Or perhaps on any carousel.

Adopted by Phi Gamma Delta fraternity, the horse has a purple mane and shaggy cream-colored legs. Norm's colors, the fraternity explained, symbolize the history and rituals of Phi Gamma Delta.

The horse is named after the fraternity's award for the best committee chairman. Norm, the brothers said, shows the University of Montana chapter's dedication to community service. And to the Missoula community.

Said Chuck Kaparich of the pony's colors: "When the project first started, I would probably have balked at the request for a purple mane. But after Larry Pirnie's pony Paint, it was easy to say 'good idea.' "

❧

big sky gaiety

Old friend
*immortalized
on carousel*

When Jeanne Joscelyn was 14, she bought a dream horse with earnings from a part-time job at a small country cafe up Lolo Creek.

Big Sky Gaiety, a registered Morgan mare, was with Joscelyn's childhood family, then her married family for 22 years before dying in February 1994. "It was so wonderful that our boys got to know her and ride her sometimes, too," Joscelyn said.

And that all of Missoula – and all who visit Missoula – can forever know Gaiety by way of the carousel horse that bears her likeness. The carousel Gaiety was adopted by Jeanne and her husband, David Joscelyn, and their business, Lube and Oil Plus.

Big Sky Gaiety was the sixth wooden horse carved for the carousel and was painted by Vanelle Nurse during a class taught by Spokane carousel artist Bette Largent.

"There is a strong resemblance between the real Gay and the carousel Gay," Joscelyn said.

The many daisies on the bridle, trappings and behind the seat of Big Sky Gaiety were a request from Joscelyn, who loved riding her mare through a pasture of daisies.

"Gay was so fun to ride," she remembered. "We have many wonderful memories. Gay was very spirited and lively, but so loveable and friendly at the same time. She loved her hay and oats, and always looked forward to a treat and some attention and petting."

❧

UNQUOTE

"*It is so very special to have the carousel Big Sky Gaiety honor the real Big Sky Gaiety. We are thankful to everyone involved with the project.*"

– Jeanne Joscelyn, pony parent

cherished angel

Cherished Angel is the carousel pony adopted by Chuck and Joyce Shepard in memory of their daughter, Carrie, who died as an infant. And it does indeed look like a little girl's horse: white and bright and flowery.

The pansies on the wooden pony's blanket and trappings were favorites of Joyce Shepard's grandmother. There is even a butterfly on the horse's right rear flank.

The cocker spaniel crouched behind the saddle memorializes the Shepard's dog, Angel.

Carver Dave Streit, who was assigned the body of Cherished Angel, used his own dog – Cooper – as a model. It was Streit's first work on a pony body, having graduated up the ranks of carvers from gargoyles to pony legs, then body work.

The same story came from Barry Swidler, who carved Cherished Angel's head, his first. Look closely at the mouth, Swidler advised. It is closed, a rarity among carousel horses.

 è

"We could not have done better."

– Dave Streit, carousel carver

MONTANA *appaloosa*

peace pony
bears handprint
of early supporter

Montana Appaloosa, the Indian peace pony on Missoula's carousel, has the real handprint of the first Carousel for Missoula Foundation president, Henry G. Bugbee.

Friends and family adopted the horse in Bugbee's honor. Then he went to work with carousel artist John Thompson, researching books and photographs of appaloosa horses.

Bugbee said he wanted his horse to honor both the state of Montana and its Native American heritage. The appaloosa was an easy choice. "An inspiring horse," he said.

To produce the red handprint on Montana Appaloosa's back right flank, Bugbee provided his own hand, dipped in paint.

At Bugbee's request, the horse carries a peace pipe rather than a bow and arrows. "I wanted a peace pony, not a war pony," he said.

Carver Alex McDonald happily obliged, visiting museums throughout western Montana to study Indian artifacts: peace pipes, shields and saddles. He, too, professed a love of appaloosa horses.

"This horse showed such workmanship," Bugbee said when work was completed. "It has received nothing but enthusiastic approval."

A peace pipe adorns Montana Appaloosa.

seattle sue

pony pays tribute
to a lost niece

Seattle Sue was adopted in memory of Susan Fisher Beckwith, the niece of Maurice and Marion Volkman.

Raised in Seattle (thus the Seattle Sue), Susan was murdered in Denver just before A Carousel for Missoula began its Adopt-A-Pony fundraiser. The Volkmans decided to memorialize her with a wooden pony, adopted in her name.

Susan was the oldest daughter of Glenn Fisher, Marion Volkman's brother. The Fisher children grew up in Missoula.

Seattle Sue's design was the work of Marion Volkman, with aid and advice from carousel creator Chuck Kaparich and artist John Thompson. Her daughter, Debbie Liberko, selected the horse's chestnut color and blue, pink and yellow saddle and trappings.

Kaparich said he learned "everything about perseverance" from Bob Homer, who carved the body of Seattle Sue. "Bob was the most teachable carver we had. He did his very best every moment he was in the shop. From a background of no woodworking at all, I don't know who was more excited, Bob or I, when I moved him to the rank of head carver."

❧

UNQUOTE

"**E**very horse was better than the one before. People really matured and grew in their abilities. But I still marvel at the early horses. Most of us had no experience, yet they are still beautiful."

– Vanelle Nurse, carousel painter

prairie rose

pony reminiscent
of that land
east of the divide

John Ruffatto and Bill Jones came from the prairies of eastern Montana, where the prairie rose grows wild. They wanted their adopted carousel pony to carry the rose – and the memories of John's days in Brockton and Bill's in Miles City.

The men adopted the carousel pony Prairie Rose with their wives, Fran Ruffatto and Karen Jones. Fran designed much of the horse and its colors.

Prairie Rose was one of the demonstration ponies at the 1992 Western Montana Fair. By Christmas of that year, the horse was finished and on display in a downtown storefront.

Sanding and priming duties for the horse fell to Gerald and Ethel Diettert, Jan Potts and Ione Briedlander.

After priming and before painting, the crew "didn't think this horse could ever look any better," Gerry Diettert remembered. "Imagine how we felt after the painters finished!"

Briedlander was so smitten with Prairie Rose that she chose it for her first ride on the carousel.

It had been her first pony to sand, she said. "Chuck (Kaparich) handed me the head and said, 'Here. You can sand this.' When I saw how beautiful I could make her, I wanted to do more."

Kaparich carved the head and neck of Prairie Rose. At the time, he was studying the work of Charles Carmel, an early-day carousel carver.

"I was really struggling with my woodworking," Kaparich said. Then, without explanation, everything became effortless, "almost like someone was guiding my hands." Kaparich has a feeling he was getting a hand from Carmel.

❧

pal's pal

famed parrot
rides upon
his trusty steed

Pal, as many a Missoula old-timer will tell you, was the parrot that lived in the Garden City Floral Co., often riding on the shoulder of owner Sam Caras.

Nowadays, a hand-carved wooden Pal rides on the back of the carousel pony adopted by Gerald A. and Ethel Caras Diettert in honor of Sam and Grace Caras. The pony's name: Pal's Pal.

The horse is decked in roses and ribbons to depict the floral shop. A card hand on the horse's chest reminds riders of Grace Caras's love of bridge.

A carousel volunteer himself, Gerald Diettert was asked to carve the legs of Pal's Pal in the winter of 1994, then the body later that spring. His wife was skeptical of his abilities, he said, "but the other carvers gave me a lot of encouragement – and ribbing."

"I finished carving a rose and asked Jim Evans for his opinion," Diettert said. Came the reply, "I always block them out like that before I start the serious carving."

Pal the parrot was the toughest part of the assignment, according to Diettert. "I spent a lot of time at Petland, looking at the parrots and collecting a sheaf of pictures."

Michael Peck carved the head and neck of Pal's Pal – and hid two signatures on the pony.

While carving the roses on the head, his daughter, Jadie, asked if she could put a ladybug on one of the petals. She did the drawing, dad the carving.

Since Pal's hooves had no frogs (the horny pads on the sole of horses' hooves), Peck asked if he could put a real frog on one hoof. The Diettert family obliged. Look closely and you will find the carousel's only frog.

❧

"Since Pal's Pal is not a jumper, I've noticed that babies, little kids and older people like to ride on him. That makes me feel good that he's there for people who may be a little apprehensive about riding."

— **Michael Peck, carousel carver**

A shiny parrot rides high on Pal's Pal.

paint

*p*ainter puts
fresh spin
on western theme

*i*t's OK, artist Larry Pirnie says, for cowboys to have purple hair. And for horses to be green or orange – or green, orange, pink, blue and yellow.

Because when Pirnie picks up the paints in his Missoula studio each morning, the kid inside him paints what he wants to paint. And when Pirnie designed his pony for the carousel, the kid wanted a horse in full stride – in full color.

The result was Paint, the much-colored, much-adored carousel horse.

"I have always seen the running horse as an ever-changing array of electric colors," Pirnie said. "I fantasize jumping on its back, and hanging on with great joy as it takes me on endless adventures."

"My relationship with the horse has nothing to do with reality," Pirnie advised. "The colors and their arrangement encourage all that see it into their own fantasies."

Paint is unmistakable Pirnie, a tribute to the wild, child-like style that has made Pirnie's paintings and cutouts of cowboys, cows, horses and bison favorites of art collectors cross-country.

"It really is special to have such an unorthodox design on our carousel," said carver Barry Swidler.

The response has run the range from head-wagging "nos" to head-bobbing "yeses," much as it is to all of Pirnie's productions.

"People don't have heavy, logical discussions about my work," he said. "They get in front of it, and they say, 'Ick!' or they say, 'I love it.' Both of which are fine with me."

Swidler, the carver, is of the school that loves it. "And I've heard many, many children say they like Paint the best. I never imagined there would be a horse like him on our carousel. I'm just so pleased he is there."

❧

UNQUOTE

"*I would bet Paint is the most loved horse of all.*"

– **Barry Swidler, carousel carver**

midnight rose

neighbors
*to the north
brought this friend*

*t*hey were just being neighborly, say six Canadian carvers who created the carousel pony Midnight Rose as a gift to Missoula.

"It was something we wanted to do for our friends south of the border," said carver Al Kapusta, who learned of Missoula's carousel-in-the-making while attending a wood-carving seminar at the University of Montana, then recruited five friends back home in Calgary, Alberta, to be his pony-carving crew.

All were attracted by the chance to be part of history: Missoula's was the first completely hand-carved wooden carousel produced in North America since the Depression.

And each looked upon the project as a "very neighborly act," Kapusta said.

None of the Albertans had ever before carved anything larger than birds, decoys, dogs or caricatures. But they consulted library books and small-scale models of horses – and soon, Kapusta said, Midnight Rose started to take shape.

The only of Missoula's carousel horses not carved in Missoula, Midnight Rose has a high-tossed head, curly mane and thick neck. It is the adopted pony of First Interstate Bank, which dedicated the horse to the memory of Pat Davis, a bank employee killed in a horseback riding accident in 1992.

First Interstate provided the design and color scheme. Kapusta's crew did the carving, sanding, priming and painting.

As their signature, the Canadians carved a tiny cowboy's head and an Alberta rose on the horse's right rear flank. They also named the pony – Midnight for its shiny black coat (a surprise, Kapusta said, as the carvers had envisioned their creation as a white horse) and Rose for the Alberta rose.

ઢ

A cowboy's head and an Alberta rose mark the Canadian influence on Midnight Rose.

marguerite

pony packs
a feminine
touch

Marguerite is "the girlie horse" on Missoula's carousel.

It is, for starters, a filly, light coated and golden maned.

It was adopted by the Missoula chapter of the Philanthropic Educational Organization (PEO's), an all-female group.

And it was the only horse on the carousel carved entirely by women.

Cyndi Joslyn, who painted some of the carousel's most stunning ponies, carved the head and neck of Marguerite. She was, in fact, the only woman on the carousel crew to carve a pony head, the most demanding job.

Joslyn's signature is hidden on Marguerite's halter. There, encircled in gold, you'll find the outline of a Santa Claus. Joslyn carves Santas as a hobby, and increasingly as a business. She also hid two tiny Santa faces (in place of leaves) on one of the carousel's hand-carved mirrors.

Rebecca Swindle carved Marguerite's body, with its delicate saddle and daisies on the trappings. Kathy Lynch, a PEO member, painted the pony. (The daisy is the PEO flower. And Marguerite is the name of a white daisy.)

&

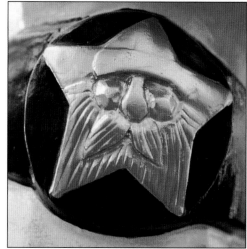

Cyndi Joslyn signed Marguerite with a Santa.

"The quietness and rhythm of carving appeal to me. And the really intense focus. You have to focus closely or you'll hurt yourself."

– Cyndi Joslyn, carousel carver

leo the lionheart

Jim Dunlap calls himself the "one-armed carver of Leo the Lionheart." Which he was.

After a serious injury to his arm in January 1994, Dunlap started work on the Missoula Lions Clubs' horse – Leo the Lionheart. The work quickly became "a creative process for Leo and a therapeutic one for me," Dunlap remembered.

"When I see Leo proudly making his rounds with a joyful rider, I think about how we got better together. I suspect the same is true for all of us who were fortunate enough to work on the carousel. In one way or another, we all got better together."

Leo is painted in Lions Club blue and gold, and displays the club emblem on its chest. (The paint job is the work of Marlies Borchers.) Five lion heads are spaced around the saddle and blanket.

The young lion faces on the romance side – the for-show side – of the horse wear favorite expressions of Dunlap's grandchildren, Sam and Alex. Look closely for clues to their personalities.

Five lion heads adorn Leo the Lionheart.

83

koko

*pony's a cowpoke
with roots
in the county*

*r*ealizing that individually they likely could not afford to adopt a pony on the carousel, Missoula County employees collected $2,500 from among their ranks.

The result: Koko, a western cow pony, adopted and designed by county workers. "And we are all very devoted to this little pony," said Sandra "Sam" Gursky. "It was exciting for us, as a group, to be able to participate in such a wonderful project."

Jack Rennaker at the Missoula County Sheriff's Department selected the name Koko. All agreed. A committee of three worked on the design, adding some "flash" with the southwestern saddle and bridle.

Carving duties fell to Jerry Covault, himself a lifelong public servant and U.S. Forest Service retiree. He particularly liked the chocolate brown pony because it was so realistic, reminding him of his boyhood on a farm in Iowa.

You'll find Covault's "signature" on the cantle of Koko's saddle: a fire-breathing dragon. It is, Covault said, a tribute to his grandson, Sam, whose favorite stuffed animal is a black dragon puppet named Puff.

(Covault's family, in turn, paid tribute to him by adopting a tune in his name on the carousel band organ: "Puff the Magic Dragon.")

Historically, carousel carvers were not allowed to sign their work, for fear they would become famous and be hired away by a competing factory. Instead, they left hidden "signatures."

Missoula's volunteer carvers honored that tradition on their ponies. Thus, Covault's secret dragon.

☙

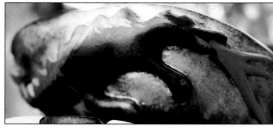

A dragon rides Koko as a tribute to a carver's grandson.

evansgone

eleven children
inspire a pony
for a family

arvin and Virginia Horner raised 11 children in a house on Evans Street, in Missoula's university district. When the children grew up and left home, though, the big house on Evans was sold.

Thus, Evansgone – the Horner family horse on Missoula's carousel.

A palomino at the request of Virginia Horner, Evansgone is modeled after a carved horse in Madrid, Spain. Carousel artists and carvers consulted a picture of the Spanish horse in rendering their own. The riding saddle also is Spanish, with the addition of the Horner family crest.

"There is no story behind the horse. We just thought it was a great idea to begin with and got swept up in the excitement," Virginia Horner said.

The color around Evansgone's neck was a favorite of the late Hilda Johnson, grandmother to the Horner children and Virginia Horner's mother. Mrs. Johnson died in 1994 at age 97.

The 11 stones on the pony's breast collar are the birthstones of the children. Since all 11 attended and graduated from Loyola Sacred Heart High School, the school colors were used for the checkered saddle blanket and the rollup behind the saddle.

Each Horner child received a miniature carving of the horse; each of the 23 grandchildren took turns riding Evansgone during its first summer on the platform.

Carver Ron Gaumer said he was overwhelmed when Chuck Kaparich handed him the block of wood intended for Evansgone's body. "I thought, 'Where do I start?' " he said. "Not being an artist and with very little experience with wood carving, I was hesitant. However, once the chisel and mallet began rounding the block, the confidence began to build."

❧

bud

pony is flavored
*with spice
of a clydesdale*

*b*ud was the longest and best-kept secret in Watkins family history.

A Clydesdale pony, Bud was a Christmas present from the Watkins children to their parents, Bunts and June Watkins.

"My mother periodically mentioned how she would like to adopt a horse, and we were so relieved when she didn't follow through," said daughter Debbie Beaudette. "Although, His and Her horses would have been OK, too."

Debbie and her sister Dian Schmidt were volunteer carvers for the carousel; their first task after finishing the prerequisite mirror frame were Bud's two front legs.

"The whole experience of being a volunteer carver and meeting so many wonderful people, most of whom we never would have had the chance to know, has been one of life's greatest enjoyments," Debbie said.

Bud is named and designed as a tribute to the Watkins family's 40-year affiliation with Anheuser-Busch and Budweiser as beer distributors.

Look on the back of Bud, just behind the saddle, for the Eagle and A emblem of Anheuser-Busch.

Bud is the only draft horse on Missoula's carousel, and one of only two ponies wearing blinders.

❧

A M E R I C A N

beauty

this horse
pays tribute
to Caras family

american Beauty, the carousel pony, is a celebration of the lives of Jim and Jean Caras – whose family adopted the pony in their honor.

The American Beauty rose, daughter Louise Caras said, is probably the most popular and best known variety of red rose. "To us, it symbolizes Jim's success in the floral business he founded (Garden City Floral and Nursery), as well as his great pride in being an American."

The carousel pony has cascades of red roses on its neck and rump, each carved separately and attached to the body with wooden dowels. Cyndi Joslyn and Bette Largent were responsible for the painstaking paint job, Phil Bain for the carving.

Joslyn told a tale of mystery about American Beauty: As she was painting the horse, she noticed one rose on the neck had no leaves. She showed carver Bain, who said it looked fine. Overnight, two wooden leaves appeared on the rose. No one ever took credit for their creation.

"This was the only horse I carved alone," Bain said. "I know several of the Caras family, so it was a pleasure to help represent their history."

Jim Caras came to the United States from Greece in 1905. He became a U.S. citizen, served in the Army in World War I, and felt a great love and loyalty for his adopted country.

The Caras family pony carries both the American flag and the Greek flag and Greek key design. Also among the adornments are the Masonic, Eastern Star and Kiwanis emblems, in honor of Jim's and Jean's civic ties.

Look on American Beauty's breast collar to find the faces of the Caras children: James, Janet, Irene and George.

"*Jim and Jean would be very proud and happy to know they were part of this splendid accomplishment – and that it is here in Caras Park!*"

– Louise Caras, pony parent

sweet sue

gentle horse
*inspired
carousel pony*

Sweet Sue – the "real" Sue – was ever so sweet. "The only malicious thing I ever saw her do was to carefully sidestep onto the foot of a vet who was drawing her blood," said Mary Hall, the horse's owner and companion for 12 years.

The real Sue died in January 1995 (at age 40-plus), but is memorialized in a jet black carousel pony that bears her name. The two look much alike, said Hall.

Sweet Sue was the fifth horse carved for Missoula's carousel by Chuck Kaparich.

"It's so nice to have a permanent connection to the community. And to Sweet Sue," Hall said.

Sue was a quarter horse, with maybe some draft horse in her. Her back feet were white; a blaze decorated her face.

For years, Sweet Sue boarded in the upper Rattlesnake pasture of Helen Cipolato. She was the one horse on the place allowed to wander and trim the grass. Every once in a while, she'd escape, once to visit some mules she had met across the fencerow.

"I had taken one riding lesson when I got Sue, but she was never a bit of trouble," said Hall, who was given the horse by a breeder at a dog show. "She was a good, sweet horse."

❧

"Sweet Sue was the first horse my wife and I worked on. We helped sand it, then Ethel and I primed it. It looked like a marble statue!"

– Gerald Diettert, carousel sander

cannonball

an outfitter's
hard-charger
is pony's namesake

*f*or 21 years the lead horse for outfitter Smoke Elser's pack string, Cannonball probably traveled 45,000 miles in the Bob Marshall Wilderness.

"All summer and fall every year, I rode him," Elser said. "I called him Cannonball because he was chargin' – a real cannonball right down the trail, flying along."

"I have a hundred pictures of old Cannonball on the trail. He had quite a history," Elser said.

When Elser taught packing classes, Cannonball was his demonstration horse, picking up his feet on command, staying put for funny loads, letting Elser pick up two of his legs at the same time.

Elser rode Cannonball, a saddlebred-thoroughbred combination, until the horse was 25, then let him spend the rest of his years in a Rattlesnake Valley pasture. Cannonball died at age 34, the same year work began on Missoula's carousel.

When, during a Rotary Club lunch one day, conversation turned to a name for the club's adopted carousel horse, Elser had a quick answer: "Let's call him Cannonball."

"I had just lost my horse," he remembered. "And I thought he was deserving."

The Rotary Clubs of Missoula horse does not resemble the actual Cannonball. The "real" horse was a sorrel with white stocking feet and a crooked stripe down the front of his nose. The carousel horse is a white steed with gold armor, the Rotary emblem, and royal blue and maroon trappings.

❧

A L T R U S A

chariot

e*veryone can ride
in this blue-and-
gold beauty*

*t*heresa Cox watched thousands of riders – actually, more than 125,000 – spin up and down, round and round Missoula's carousel in its first summer of operation.

But none touched her more than the wheelchair-bound riders, some of whom asked to be lifted onto horses, others of whom wheeled their chair into one of two specially designed chariots.

"They just beamed," said Cox, the carousel's first director. One married couple, both in wheelchairs, came to the carousel almost every day, she said.

The chariots were similarly popular with mothers of new babies and some older riders.

The carousel's blue and gold, "quilted" chariot was adopted by Altrusa International Club of Missoula. Altrusa Club members have always been concerned about people with disabilities, said member Mary Ball. The chariot seemed like a natural service project.

Blue and gold are the club colors; Altrusa emblems decorate the wheel spokes and front of the chariot.

❧

"**I** *am continually in awe of the people who actually did the work of creating this carousel. I am very, very grateful to them all.*"

**– Theresa Cox, executive director,
A Carousel for Missoula**

EAGLE

chariot

e*verything about this gem challenged the carver*

*J*im Story was one of the few Carousel for Missoula carvers who was a carver before there was a carousel.

Needless to say, he was put to work right away. And when he volunteered to carve the eagle chariot, he got the assignment. Quickly.

There were plenty of problems in bringing the spectacular chariot to completion. How do you attach the massive bald eagle to the chariot? Story wondered. How do you curve the wings? How do you create a basket effect for the chariot itself?

For each question, though, Story found an answer. The process took two years and called upon all his experience as an amateur carver and heavy construction worker. (He spent 45-plus years building the big dams and powerhouses of the western United States.)

The chariot's basket weave was created out of oak, split to thin strips which Story hot-steamed, then bent around dowels. The eagle was fit to the chariot piece by piece, with each piece glued to the next until the body of the bird fit onto and around the chariot.

The carving, too, was done a piece at a time, Story said. "I carved the fish first, then the talons that fit over the fish, then the legs and body, ending up with the head."

The fisherman on the side of the chariot was Story's whimsy – his carver's signature. "I like that he's fishing and having this tug of war with the eagle and the fish," he said. And yes, that's a real piece of a fishing pole in the angler's grasp and real fishing line from pole to fish's mouth.

Inside the chariot, you'll find the name "Carol" carved discreetly (but distinctly) into the basket. That's the name of Story's niece, disabled since birth, and a tribute to all those in wheelchairs who ride the carousel.

The chariot was adopted by the Missoula Building Industry Association. The eagle is a symbol of the association's umbrella group, the National Association of Homebuilders.

❧

"*I worry about that eagle. Every time I visit the carousel, I look to make sure all the pieces are still intact.*"

– Jim Story, carousel carver

A foundling frame

in 1918, craftsmen at the Herschell-Spillman carousel factory in North Tonawanda, N.Y., produced a 40-foot, 14-bay, three-row, steam-powered carousel.

Today, the mechanical workings of that carousel sit on the banks of the Clark Fork River in Missoula, spinning 38 hand-carved wooden ponies and two chariots.

In between, there were many incarnations for the carousel frame – some of which remain a mystery.

The workings of Missoula's carousel passed through the doors of the Herschell-Spillman factory during the heyday of hand-carved carousels. At the time, the factory produced nearly one carousel a day.

Little is known of the frame's first 40

Carver and lead mechanic Jack Gillespie lubes a bearing. "I love craftsmanship," he says. "It's a dying thing. Every single detail of this carousel is exactly correct."

years. Carousel creator Chuck Kaparich was only able to trace it to the 1950s and a storage shed in San Francisco.

About 1959, the carousel was purchased by Bob Anderson and installed at Incline Village, Nev., near Lake Tahoe, where the television series "Bonanza" was filmed. Throughout the series' filming,

the Ponderosa Ranch was a popular tourist attraction; in fact, more than 300,000 people a year still visit the ranch.

Kaparich has photographs of Anderson's carousel – and of "Bonanza" star Lorne Greene hoisting a young child onto one of the carousel creatures.

Anderson sold the carousel at auction in 1983. The animals went separately, each to the highest bidder. The old frame went to Montana.

Kaparich found the pieces for his machine by accident. An antique dealer in the Bitterroot Valley told him of an old frame piled behind a building in Polson. It was practically worthless, the man warned.

Kaparich grabbed a telephone, called his boss to say he wouldn't be back for the afternoon and headed north. In Polson, behind the Miracle of America Museum, were the guts of a carousel, bent and rusting and covered in snow.

Kaparich felt like a kid on Christmas

morning.

"He knew what he was looking at and I could tell he would do something with it," said Gil Mangels, the museum's owner. Mangels had bought the workings from an antique store in Kalispell as part of a deal that included a Herschell park train.

Take the frame and you can buy the train, Mangels was told.

Kaparich and Mangels negotiated a deal on the spot, writing the terms on a greasy piece of notepaper:

"I, Gil Mangels, agree to sell to Chuck Kaparich of 503 Connell, Missoula, Montana, a carousel frame, including seven-piece sectional gear, 14 sweeps, 11 cranks, drop rods and all gears in my possession for the sum of $3,000. $500 paid in hand October 28 and $2,500 on November 3 when carousel is picked up."

Kaparich drove back to Missoula smiling and burst into the house to deliver the news to his wife, Beth.

I've bought a carousel, he

David "Mac" MacInnes, a long-time machinist for the Burlington Northern and Northern Pacific railroads, retired 19 years ago. His expertise was required to pour bearings and assemble the works. Despite the fact that the frame was a pile of pieces, MacInnes says the mechanics had few problems with assembly: "It was just a matter of fitting things together."

proclaimed. I thought you were buying a car, came the reply. Well . . .

That was in 1991.

It took four years for Kaparich and a volunteer crew of 12 machinists, mechanics and electricians to restore the mechanism to better-than-new condition, pouring new babbit bearings, remanufacturing parts and

tracking down missing pieces.

A much-needed crankshaft was located in Cincinnati, Ohio, for $125. Cost to ship it to Missoula: $135. "The net result: the Missoula carousel," said Kaparich.

It was all, Kaparich said, learn as you go. He read everything he could about carousels, looking for clues to their assembly. One volunteer

later admitted that he had no idea what he was doing for the first two years.

One wonderful stroke of luck, in Kaparich's words, was his meeting Ed Widger, who had worked at the Herschell-Spillman factory and was "a carousel encyclopedia."

Another was a meeting arranged by one of Kaparich's neighbors. "Chuck," said the neighbor, "I'd like you to meet Mac. He worked with me on the railroad."

"Pleased to meet you," Kaparich replied.

"I didn't know at the time, but with the firm handshake of Mac MacInnes, I was introduced to the finest machinist I have ever known. And to the finest gentleman," he said. "Every week, we relied heavily on the skills and expertise of this incredibly wise and talented man."

Also on the mechanical crew were: Jim Brown, Bill Evans, Kent Jones, Mike Alvernaz, Steve Tillotson, Jack Gillespie, Sam Johnson and Frank Wryn.

pipe dreams

Scott Olson, gaviman.

Meet Scott Olson, gaviman. You'll find him, more days than not, tending the instrument he has humbly proclaimed the finest military band organ ever built. "It is like no other," says Olson, a gaviman in the tradition of the craftsmen who once tended gavioli organs for traveling carnivals.

The band organ in the Carousel for Missoula building is, in fact, America's largest carousel band organ.

Built to Missoula's specifications at Don Stinson's band organ company in Bellefontaine, Ohio, the machine was 1-1/2 years in the making and cost $65,000.

It is equally impressive on paper and in operation.

Four-hundred pipes duplicate the sounds of 23 instruments and 45 musicians: saxophones, flutes, piccolos, violins, viola, bass drum, snare drum, wood block and cymbal, a tiny cast bell and a shiny chrome xylophone.

The smallest pipe is 2 inches, the longest 10 feet. The wood is yellow poplar and maple, with maple caps on the clarinet row.

The sound they produce is a marvel to Olson, a Missoula organ repairman who thrice traveled to Ohio to watch over the construction and who admits to having hoped for a band organ of his own since the age of 4.

"Finally, it's here," he said when the organ arrived – with just two pipes out of tune – in August 1994.

Don Stinson himself traveled to Missoula to tune his creation the day before the carousel opened to the public. "This community should be proud. Very, very proud," he said.

"This – this organ and this carousel – is one in a million."

Missoula's band organ plays music punched onto rolls which look and work like player piano rolls. A search by Olson turned up both American-made rolls with lots of oom-pah-pahs, in the style of John Philip Sousa, and European rolls that are more melodic.

Several new music rolls also were created just for the carousel, featuring music "adopted" by local donors: the University of Montana fight song, "Anything Goes" and "All Right Now," among others.

No less impressive is the 8-foot-high, 17-foot-wide, hand-carved wooden facade that encloses the organ.

The work of volunteer carver Glenn Watters, the organ facade took as long to complete as did the organ itself.

Watters' creation is replete with bright-colored dragons (their tails encircle the drums), knights whose steeds move up and down to the music, a mountain cragg and castle (and two more dragons) and a tiny sword (fashioned after a Swiss army knife) in a stone (of wood).

Only the xylophone and the tiny chrome bell remain in view – "for the kids," Watters said.

❧

THAT
volunteer
SPIRIT

Hundreds donated time and money and spirit to A Carousel for Missoula. Here's a glimpse at a few who helped make it happen.

THERESA COX

theresa Cox remembers well the first day she saw one of Chuck Kaparich's hand-carved wooden carousel ponies. And her reaction: "There's nothing I can do that will help those people."

Then someone suggested the carousel campaign needed a newsletter. And another someone suggested Cox, who already produced newsletters for her children's school, her church and paying customers.

"They needed me," she said.

Thus began an association that culminated in the Carousel for Missoula Foundation naming Cox as the carousel's first executive director in June 1995.

In her first summer, Cox counted 125,000 riders – not counting those who attended 100 birthday parties, two weddings and countless brunches and receptions.

"We had no mechanical failures, no injuries and only three people got sick," she said. "It was a very, very good summer. For us all."

STEVE WEILER

Just days after Chuck Kaparich proposed A Carousel for Missoula to city officials, Steve Weiler happened by the carver's exhibit at the Western Montana Fair.

There were four horses, all designed and carved by Kaparich: an Indian pony, a traditional carousel horse, a knight's charger and a Montana bucking bronco.

Weiler wanted in.

The manager at Missoula Ace Hardware, Weiler was a student in the first carving class Kaparich taught that next winter, hoping to train and recruit carousel carvers. They made gargoyles, preludes to the larger ponies.

Weiler still wanted in.

"We graduated to horse legs, then bodies, then necks and finally heads," he remembered. "We'd meet at Chuck's once a week, and I carved a lot at home."

Weiler carved the neck and head of Red Ribbons, one of the early-favorite carousel horses. He also did the body of Prairie Rose. Then Kaparich gave him full responsibility for Hard Hat, the Pew family horse. So pleased was the family

with the finished product that they wanted to make a donation to the carousel in Weiler's name.

The highest compliment, though, came when Kaparich asked him to carve the lead horse – Columbia Belle, an ornately decorated creature – the most embellished of any of the carousel horses.

Weiler spent nine months on the horse, carrying parts around with him to ask

the opinion of adopters, family and friends.

"Every step of the way, this project has been as good as we could make it," Weiler said. "We always did the best we could do. The best building. The best band organ. The best of everything."

❧

CYNDI JOSLYN

Cyndi Joslyn is, by her own admission, just about the biggest carousel junkie in Missoula.

In July of 1994, she quit her job at a Missoula podiatrist's office to work full time on the carousel. For free.

"There I was, a single mother quitting a sure thing to work as a volunteer for a year," Joslyn said. "But I knew what I was doing. And if I'd known it was so much fun, I would have done it sooner."

For nine weeks that first summer, Joslyn painted the yellow, red and green trim inside the carousel building. Then she painted ponies. And carved and sanded ponies. And volunteered in the gift shop. And, in April of 1995, accepted a paid job as the gift shop manager.

She was the only woman in the carousel crew to carve the head of a horse – the most-demanding job. Joslyn carved the head and neck of Marguerite, the light-coated, daisy-maned horse adopted by the Missoula Philanthropic

KURT WILSON

Educational Organization (PEO's).

(Marguerite was, in fact, the only horse on the carousel carved entirely by women. Becca Swindle of Victor carved the body.)

Joslyn's hand-carved Santas – pins and statues – also became early mainstays in the carousel gift shop. One of her more intricate creations sold for $1,500 at the carousel's fund-raising auction in April 1994. A second bidder offered another $1,500 if Joslyn would carve another Santa.

Joslyn tried to take the first carousel carving class offered by Kaparich the winter of 1992, but called too late. "Fifteen minutes after the vo-tech opened," she recalled, "there were already 25 people on the waiting list."

She missed the second class because of eye surgery, so begged her way onto the carving crew.

"I like the animal and the artform," she said. "My love of horses initially attracted me to the carousel." Later, she added, she was intrigued by the "pure communism" of the project: "everyone working for the good of the community, without financial gain, without prima donnas."

≈

JOHN THOMPSON

John Thompson lived with a paintbrush in hand while the carousel was being built. Yet he says, "I am not a painter."

He is, in fact, a printmaker. But as the carousel project got under way, Thompson became the artist in residence, sketching and designing horses, designing a fantasy castle scene for the organ, painting whimsical portraits and carving both horses and slugs.

"Chuck called me up one day and asked me: Can you draw a horse? I lied, and said I could," says Thompson. "I've been involved ever since."

Chuck Kaparich recruited Thompson early to sketch horses so that Missoula residents could see the potential of the ideas. He ended up sketching or designing all but six of the horses, working in conjunction with the people who adopted them along the way.

"It was really a lot of fun, and sometimes a challenge," said Thompson, who also learned to carve and worked on several of the carousel figures. "Some of the horses we did and redid, until the design was right."

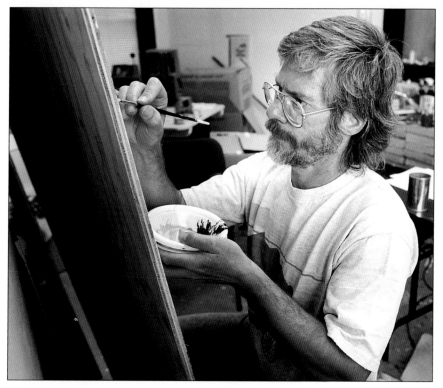

Thompson's sketches were blueprints for the hand-carved castle scene that fronts the carousel organ and the dragon that will drop rings for carousel riders.

"I have always loved reading science fiction," said the artist, whose fascination with castles, dragons and whimsy is apparent in his work. "I couldn't ask for something more fun to do."

Thompson painted all of the artist's panels that hide the center-pole machinery. They have his trademarks – castles, mystical figures, dragons – along with portraits of relatives, families, friends,

famous people from history, contemporary messages, likenesses of carousel artists and supporters – anybody he felt like including.

Look closely and you'll see a few slugs in the panels – not the slippery slimy kind, but friendly slugs that are carousel-pony-wannabes.

One of the carvers picked up a discarded piece of wood – the piece from the back of a leg – and noticed that it looked like a slug, Thompson said. Thompson took the wood home and carved a slug, then gave it carousel trappings of saddle, harness and fancy decorations.

A slug version of each carousel horse is in the works. "We'll set it up as a small carousel. It won't go up and down," Thompson said. "It will just slither."

"I wouldn't dream of not getting involved in this," said Thompson. "It was Chuck's dream, but he let all of us be part of it."

J E R R Y
C O V A U L T

*J*erry Covault is convinced the secret of life is hidden someplace in a piece of basswood.

All you have to do, he says, is keep looking.

For three years, from 1992 to 1995, Covault conducted his search as one of the volunteer woodcarvers who met each Wednesday night in Chuck Kaparich's garage in the university district.

He was drawn to the work not out of love or nostalgia for carousels, but for the woodworking and the texture and feel of the wood used to create Missoula's carousel ponies.

"My background just didn't include carousels," said Covault, retired after 33 years with the U.S. Forest Service. He could, in fact, remember but one – an unrealistic, and frankly scary carousel that came to the Guthrie County, Iowa, fair when he was a boy.

The horses, Covault said, didn't look like horses and did not, therefore, suit a farm boy.

But the wood was another matter.

During his years in the Forest Service, Covault would bring home broken handles from firefighters' Pulaskis and use them to make trinkets and children's toys in the off-season.

Never, though, did he attempt anything as big as a carousel horse. Until A Carousel for Missoula advertised for volunteer carvers.

Soon, Covault was part of Kaparich's Wednesday night carving crew, feasting on Jim Evans's homemade cookies, reveling in Dave Streit's tales of airline adventures, studying Kaparich's charisma.

"I once saw Henry Kissinger working a coliseum with thousands of people, all with his charisma," Covault said. "Chuck has the right elements of that."

Under Kaparich's tutelage, Covault carved the head of Prince, the armored pony adopted by Clark Fork Riverside residents, and the neck and body of Norm, the Phi Gamma Delta fraternity pony.

Then Kaparich assigned him all of Koko, the chocolate brown western pony adopted by Missoula County employees. All those years after grumbling that the carousel ponies at the Guthrie County Fair didn't look like horses, Covault got his chance to carve a "real" one.

And he did.

His "signature," on the saddle cantle, is an unobtrusive dragon that pays tribute to his grandson Sam, who is forever bonded to a dragon puppet named Puff. And, for forever and then some, to his grandpa.

🐟

DAVE STREIT

*i*n the years B.C. – Before Carousel – Dave Streit couldn't whittle a stick, much less carve a wooden pony. Airplanes were his venue, having flown 32 years for Continental Airlines and, before that, for Johnson Flying Service.

Then he met Jim Dunlap at a garage sale. Dunlap, a dermatologist, had just signed on as a volunteer for the Missoula carousel and was looking for carving tools. You should give it a try, too, he advised Streit.

So, as had dozens of other would-be carvers before him, Streit called carousel creator Chuck Kaparich, who put him to work sanding. Then to carving mirrors. Then horse legs. Before long, Streit was spending three nights a week, 7-10 p.m., in Kaparich's garage.

"This has been a real privilege," Streit said. "I am just thankful that I had the opportunity."

Streit's contributions include work on Cherished Angel, the pansy-and-butterfly adorned pony that memorializes the infant daughter of Chuck and Joyce Shepard. And on Patches, one of three replacement ponies.

"No one would ever have taken this assignment, had you told them everything that was involved from the start," Streit said. "There were simply thousands and thousands of details."

The secret was in taking a little piece at a time, adding this and that, and accepting "nothing second rate. Everything, absolutely everything was top-notch," he said. "We could not have done better."

❧

carousel q & a

Question: Is Chuck Kaparich a real person?

Answer: Yes, although once during construction of A Carousel for Missoula, a local radio station featured the carousel creator on its daily "Dead or Alive?" call-in contest.

Correctly identify Kaparich as dead or alive and win a pizza, the announcer said.

"Dead," guessed the caller.

"Sorry, no pizza," came the reply.

Yes, Chuck Kaparich is a real – living – Missoula person, a cabinetmaker by trade. And yes, a lot of folks have a lot of questions about Missoula's carousel.

Here are some of the most frequently asked questions, with answers by Kaparich and carousel executive director Theresa Cox.

Q: How long does each ride last?

A: Four minutes.

Q: How fast does the carousel move?

A: At top speed, the carousel travels 11 mph (or 6 rpm) on the outside row. That's fast for a carousel. Fast enough to make your hair blow back.

Q: Are there seat belts on the ponies?

A: Yes. There are leather belts with buckles and buttons.

Q: Are there ponies that don't move up and down?

A: Yes. Two, Pal's Pal and Avalon. They're located just inside from the chariots.

Q: Which direction does the carousel move?

A: Counter-clockwise. English carousels go clockwise, while American and other European carousels turn counter-clockwise. Because of the way American carousels turn, the right side – or "romance side" – of Missoula's carousel horses is more lavishly decorated than the left side. The left side of a carousel horse is called its "finance side"!

Q: Is the carousel wheelchair accessible?

A: Yes. Both chariots have seats that fold out of the way for a wheelchair. A portable ramp provides access onto the carousel platform. Handicapped riders always ride free on A Carousel for Missoula.

Q: Who owns the carousel?

A: The city of Missoula owns the carousel building in Caras Park. However, A Carousel for Missoula Foundation owns the horses, the carousel frame, the band organ and all carousel-related items.

Q: Who runs the carousel?

A: Theresa Cox is the carousel's executive director, overseeing a staff of permanent and seasonal employees. Cox answers to and was hired by the foundation board.

Q: Who gets the profit?

A: A Carousel for Missoula is a not-for-profit corporation. If money is raised in the course of regular operations, the carousel is entitled to maintain an endowment fund to pay for repair and upkeep of the carousel. Any profits over the level needed to maintain the endowment will be split with the city. The carousel has tentative plans to use its portion of any extra profits to upgrade city parks and provide artistic and academic opportunities for area students.

Q: Why are there so many dragons and gargoyles in the carousel building?

A: On the earliest European carousels, the gargoyles were in place to protect the riders' jewels. Carousels were originally toys for adults, not children – and for the rich, rather than for commoners. It was also thought the gargoyles added a note of daring to the ride.

As for the dragons. Well, Missoula carousel artist John Thompson just likes to draw dragons. All Missoula's gargoyles and dragons are friendly.

Q: Do you grease the carousel?

A: Every day. The crank shafts overhead, as well as mechanical gears powered by the electric motor are precision pieces of equipment and need constant attention and maintenance.

Q: How do you repair "well-loved" ponies?

A: There is a pony renovation shop in the carousel building, staffed – when need be – by alumni from the carving crew. Three replacement ponies (Low Bid, Santa's Pony and Patches) ride the carousel when their cousins are in for repairs.

Q: What are all those horse heads on the posts that surround the carousel?

A: Twenty horse heads sit atop the posts that ring the carousel and provide crowd control during business hours. They were made at the Anaconda

Foundry from a mold that was used by and for copper king Marcus Daly. They are a likeness of Daly's horse, Tammany. Jim Dunlap, a retired Missoula physician and former Anaconda lad, was instrumental in working with the foundry.

Q: Who made the weather vane on top of the carousel building?

A: That was the work of the carousel's volunteer mechanical crew. They fashioned the horse from quarter-inch steel. Mechanic Sam Johnson, who did the finish cut on the horse with a disc grinder and hand files, said he likes to tell people that he "carved" the first horse everybody sees as they come to the carousel.

Q: Who designed the carousel building?

A: The building was designed by Jay Kirby and Associates of Missoula. Chosen from four entrants in a contest sponsored by the Missoula Redevelopment Agency, the building design is a blend of old and new. Carousel riders alternate between inside and outside views of the building as they make the circle. The design also complements existing Caras Park structures.

Q: Who built the carousel building?

A: The building is the work of Structural Systems, Inc. Their work, Kaparich said, was "truly wonderful."

Q: Who painted all the panels in the middle of the carousel?

A: John Thompson, the carousel's resident artist, gets credit for the center pan-

els. Thompson sketched each panel to get an overall sense of the group, then drew and painted each one. It took him all winter and spring of 1995 – and several hundred hours of volunteer labor.

Q: Who are all those people on the panels?

A: Some are composites of people, including many members of artist Thompson's extended family. Several, though, bear a striking resemblance to some of the folks you may have seen carving or painting or restoring the mechnical frame or building the carousel – or hanging around wondering when their father the artist was going to be done painting! Thompson hid hundreds of little secrets in the panels. Some of them, he's keeping all to himself.

Q: What are the horses made from?

A: Basswood, which comes from linden trees.

Q: How long did it take to carve each horse?

A: Between 400 and 800 hours – just to carve. Every hour was donated to the carousel.

Q: Are the tails real horse hair?

A: Yes. Authentic horse hair was used for the tails of all but the very first horses Chuck Kaparich carved four years ago. Each tail is trimmed and groomed – and sometimes dyed another color – before being installed on the south end of the horse.